The Open University

Mathematics Foundation Course Unit 3

OPERATIONS AND MORPHISMS

Prepared by the Mathematics Foundation Course Team

Correspondence Text 3

The Open University Press

Open University courses provide a method of study for independent learners through an integrated teaching system including textual material, radio and television programmes and short residential courses. This text is one of a series that make up the correspondence element of the Mathematics Foundation Course.

The Open University's courses represent a new system of university level education. Much of the teaching material is still in a developmental stage. Courses and course materials are, therefore, kept continually under revision. It is intended to issue regular up-dating notes as and when the need arises, and new editions will be brought out when necessary.

The Open University Press Limited
Walton Hall, Bletchley, Bucks

First Published 1970
Copyright © 1970 The Open University

Printed in Great Britain by
J W Arrowsmith Ltd Bristol BS3 2NT

SBN 335 01002 4

Contents

Objectives

The principal objective of this unit is to introduce the concept of a *morphism* and the terminology required to express it.

After working through this unit you should be able to:

   (i) explain the reasons for adopting the definitions listed in the glossary;
  (ii) test a given binary operation for associativity and commutativity;
 (iii) test two given binary operations for distributivity;
  (iv) test a given function and binary operation for compatibility, and hence for the existence of a morphism;
   (v) establish whether a given morphism is a homomorphism or an isomorphism;
  (vi) for a given morphism, determine the induced binary operation on the image set;
 (vii) for a given morphism, determine the reverse mapping;
(viii) apply dimensional analysis to simple problems;
  (ix) construct examples of morphisms not given in the text.

Note

Before working through this correspondence text, make sure you have read the general introduction to the mathematics course in the Study Guide, as this explains the philosophy underlying the whole course. You should also be familiar with the section which explains how a text is constructed and the meanings attached to the stars and other symbols in the margin, as this will help you to find your way through the text.

Structural Diagram

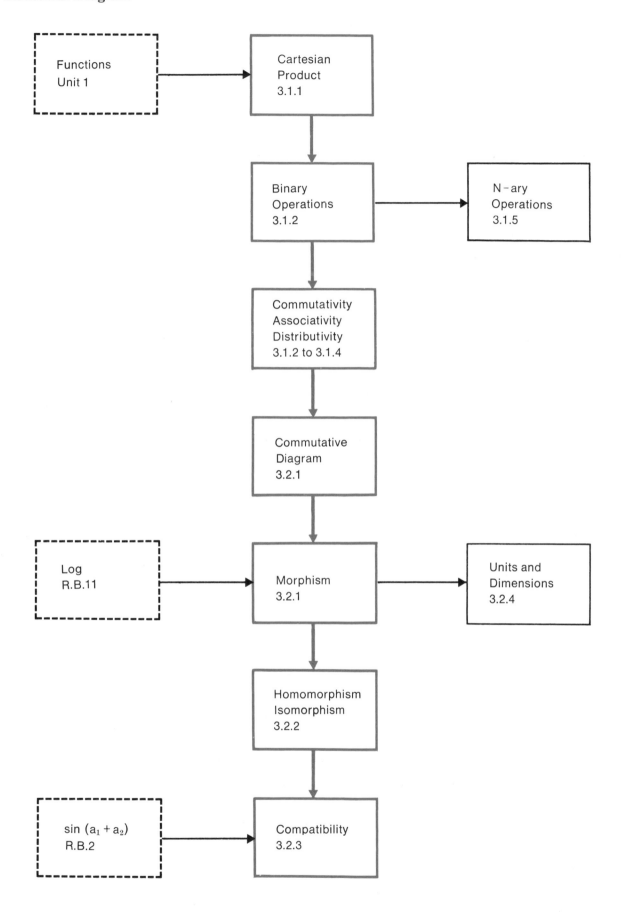

Glossary

Terms which are defined in this glossary are printed in CAPITALS.

ASSOCIATIVE BINARY OPERATION	AN ASSOCIATIVE BINARY OPERATION is a CLOSED BINARY OPERATION ∘ (say) on a set A, where $$(a_1 \circ a_2) \circ a_3 = a_1 \circ (a_2 \circ a_3)$$ for all elements of A.	11
BINARY OPERATION	A BINARY OPERATION is an operation on a set A (say), which assigns to each ordered pair $$(a_1, a_2) \in A \times A$$ a uniquely defined element b.	7
CARTESIAN PRODUCT $P \times Q$	The CARTESIAN PRODUCT of the sets P and Q is the set of all ordered pairs (p, q) where $p \in P$, $q \in Q$.	2
CLOSED BINARY OPERATION	A CLOSED BINARY OPERATION is a BINARY OPERATION ∘ (say) on a set A, for which each element b (defined above) is a member of A.	7
COMMUTATIVE BINARY OPERATION	A COMMUTATIVE BINARY OPERATION is a BINARY OPERATION ∘ (say) on a set A, where $$a_1 \circ a_2 = a_2 \circ a_1$$ for all elements of A.	9
COMMUTATIVE DIAGRAM	A COMMUTATIVE DIAGRAM is a diagram by means of which sets or elements are connected by arrows (representing operations or functions), and which permits alternative paths from the same starting point to the same finishing point.	20
COMPATIBLE	A FUNCTION f, with domain A, and a BINARY OPERATION ∘ on A are COMPATIBLE if whenever $$f(a_1) = f(a_2)$$ and $$f(a_3) = f(a_4)$$ then $$f(a_1 \circ a_3) = f(a_2 \circ a_4)$$ $a_1, a_2, a_3, a_4 \in A$.	32
DIMENSIONS	The DIMENSIONS of a physical quantity (in the context of this unit) are the symbols $$M^\alpha \quad L^\beta \quad T^\gamma$$ where M, L, T stand for mass, length and time respectively, and α, β, γ have appropriate numerical values.	37
DISTRIBUTIVE BINARY OPERATION	A DISTRIBUTIVE BINARY OPERATION is a BINARY OPERATION which is both LEFT- AND RIGHT-DISTRIBUTIVE.	14
FUNCTION	A subset of $P \times Q$ defines a FUNCTION from P to Q if each element of P appears in the first term of an ordered pair of the subset once and once only.	3
HOMOMORPHISM	A HOMOMORPHISM is a MORPHISM for which the FUNCTION f is many–one.	28
INDUCED BINARY OPERATION	The INDUCED BINARY OPERATION is the operation on the image set of a MORPHISM.	34

Page

ISOMORPHISM	An ISOMORPHISM is a MORPHISM for which the FUNCTION f is one–one.	28
LEFT-DISTRIBUTIVE BINARY OPERATION	If two CLOSED BINARY OPERATIONS, $\square$ and $\circ$ (say), satisfy	13

$$a_1 \square (a_2 \circ a_3) = (a_1 \square a_2) \circ (a_1 \square a_3)$$

for all elements of A, then the operation $\square$ is LEFT-DISTRIBUTIVE over the operation $\circ$.

MAPPING	A subset of $P \times Q$ defines a MAPPING from P to Q if every element of P appears as the first term of at least one ordered pair of the subset.	3
MATHEMATICAL MODEL	A MATHEMATICAL MODEL is a mathematical structure which represents certain specific features of the physical world.	x, 18
MORPHISM	A MORPHISM is a FUNCTION $f:(A, \circ) \longmapsto (f(A), \square)$ such that	25

$$f(a_1) \square f(a_2) = f(a_1 \circ a_2)$$

for all $a_1, a_2 \in A$.

N-ARY OPERATION	An N-ARY OPERATION is an operation on a set which operates on an ordered N-tuple of elements of that set.	15
RIGHT-DISTRIBUTIVE BINARY OPERATION	If two CLOSED BINARY OPERATIONS, $\square$ and $\circ$ (say) satisfy	14

$$(a_1 \circ a_2) \square a_3 = (a_1 \square a_3) \circ (a_2 \square a_3)$$

for all elements of A, then the operation $\square$ is RIGHT-DISTRIBUTIVE over the operation $\circ$.

TERNARY OPERATION	A TERNARY OPERATION is an operation on a set which operates on an ordered triple of elements of that set.	15
UNARY OPERATION	A UNARY OPERATION is an operation on a set which operates on only one element of that set at a time.	15

Notation

Bibliography

C. B. Allendoerfer and C. O. Oakley, *Principles of Mathematics*, 2nd ed. (McGraw-Hill, 1963).
The basic ideas of operations on the real numbers are discussed in Chapter 2. (The support given by this book to *Unit 3* is, however, fairly slight. We include it because it was recommended for *Unit 1* and will be recommended for some subsequent units.)

S. MacLane and G. Birkhoff, *Algebra*, (Macmillan, 1967).
All the concepts of this unit appear in Chapters 1 and 2. This is a difficult book, however, for first year students, but if you feel thoroughly at home with our material, you may find time spent with this book rewarding.

S. M. Selby and L. Sweet, *Sets, Relations, Functions*, (McGraw-Hill, 1963). The ideas of operations on a set, Cartesian product and isomorphism appear in this book together with considerable material not directly related to this unit but useful for other areas of the Foundation Course.

3.0 INTRODUCTION

Much of the history of science is a history of the quest for underlying and unifying theories which will enable man to explain his physical surroundings as they are experienced at any given moment of time, and to predict what these surroundings are likely to be in the future. Mathematics is no exception, and the quest for unifying concepts which will have practical application in several branches of mathematics plays an important role in research. Some of these concepts are of particular value in mathematics education.

It is because of the importance of its unifying role in mathematics that we selected the concept of *function* as the central theme of our first unit. We shall now be taking up this concept again and extending it by the introduction of the concept of *binary operation*. These two unifying concepts are very closely related to each other, and we shall be seeing how they combine to give us a rather more complex, though still fundamental, concept which we call a *morphism*.

To give you here just a flavour of this concept, consider what happens when you discover that your car needs oil. Perhaps you pour in a litre and check the level, only to find that a litre is not quite enough. So you pour in a further half-litre. If you think of the arithmetic of this, then you arrive at the obvious addition sum:

$$1 + \tfrac{1}{2} = 1\tfrac{1}{2}$$

This arithmetic represents what you have done with your car by using a mapping,

$$m : \text{quantity of oil} \longmapsto \text{numerical value in litres}$$

The domain of the mapping is a set of quantities of oil which can be combined by pouring into a single container, and the operation of addition on the codomain corresponds to the combination of quantities of oil. We can draw a diagram to represent this as follows:

You have a choice of two different paths from top left to bottom right, which indicates that you can either *pour together* and then do the mapping *m*, or first do the mapping and then *add*. We have shown the first of these paths in black and the second in red. In a loose sort of way we can say that not only does *m* map quantities of oil to numbers, but it also maps the operation of *pouring together* to the operation of *addition*.

This is a very trivial example, but the general concept has important and far-reaching implications.

We are going to ask you to spend some time in coming to grips with the morphism concept, because you will find that it is a recurring theme throughout mathematics. In this unit we shall introduce you to the concept and help you to see how it can illuminate the notion of a mathematical model. By a mathematical model we mean simply a mathematical structure which represents certain specific features of the physical world. Thus in the oil example, we say the numbers model quantities of oil and their addition models pouring oil together. When we look for a mathematical model, we want it to represent as faithfully as possible some physical or some other mathematical situation. Our search for the right model can be very much assisted if we understand the features that are common to all models, and know the kinds of question to which we should be seeking answers. You will find that the morphism concept highlights these common features and suggests just the right kind of questions to ask.

This, then, is a fundamental unit of the course and provides part of the foundations upon which much of the course will be constructed. As we refer to the concepts of function, binary operation and morphism again and again throughout subsequent units, your understanding of these concepts and their unifying role in mathematics will be reinforced, and we are confident that our inclusion of them as the basis for two early units will prove to have been of great value to you in your voyage of discovery round the "islands" which are the various specialized topics in mathematics.

3.1 OPERATIONS

3.1.0 Introduction

In this section we shall discuss the idea of *operations on a set*, examples of which you will have encountered many times, e.g. the operation of *addition* on the set of real numbers.

Intuitively, we think of an operation as something which *produces a result*. This is a perfectly satisfactory starting point for our thoughts, though, as usual in mathematics, we shall find that we need to be a little more precise when we come to give our formal definition.

In fact, we shall begin by looking back to our first correspondence text and giving you definitions of mapping and function based on work done there, but from a slightly different stand-point. This approach will link particularly well with functions whose domain is a set of ordered pairs and thus lead in to our formal definition of an operation. It will also serve as revision.

We shall see that the idea of a function and the idea of an operation are closely allied. Indeed, we shall see that this is an instance, so often encountered in mathematics, where we simply look at one and the same thing from two different stand-points. This reflects the natural way in which situations arise: a situation may lead more naturally to one mathematical formulation than to another, and for economy of mathematical effort we must be able to see through the particular formulation to the intrinsic mathematics which we may have met before when it arose from some apparently quite different situation.

3.1.1 The Cartesian Product of Two Sets

In *Unit 1, Functions*, you encountered mappings from one set to another, such as the mapping m from

$$A = \{a, b, c\}$$

to

$$B = \{1, 2, 3\}$$

illustrated by

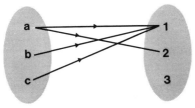

As we saw in *Unit 1*, we can just as easily represent the mapping by the set of ordered pairs,

$$\{(a, 1), (a, 2), (b, 1), (c, 1)\}$$

or by the diagram

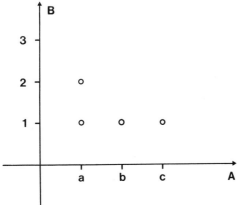

Any mapping from A to B corresponds to a set of ordered pairs, and such a set must be a subset of the set of all possible ordered pairs,

$$\{(a, 1), (a, 2), (a, 3), (b, 1), (b, 2), (b, 3), (c, 1), (c, 2), (c, 3)\}$$

However, our definition of mapping in *Unit 1* is such that not every subset of the set of all possible ordered pairs will define a mapping.

Exercise 1

Exercise 1
(5 minutes)

If you need to refresh your memory, re-read the definition of mapping on page 12 of *Unit 1* and then say which of the following sets define mappings from the set A to the set B, where

$$A = \{a, b, c\}$$

and

$$B = \{1, 2, 3\}$$

(i) $\{(a, 1), (b, 2), (c, 3)\}$

(ii) $\{(a, 1), (a, 2), (a, 3)\}$;

(iii) $\{(a, 1), (a, 3), (b, 2), (b, 1), (c, 3)\}$;

(iv) $\{(a, 1), (b, 1), (c, 2)\}$.

Which of these mappings are functions?   ■

Any mapping from a set P to a set Q will correspond to a set of ordered pairs. The first element of each pair will belong to P, and the second element to Q. The set of ordered pairs will be a subset of the set of all possible pairs (p, q) where $p \in P$ and $q \in Q$. If we call this *set of all possible pairs S*, we have

Main Text
* * *

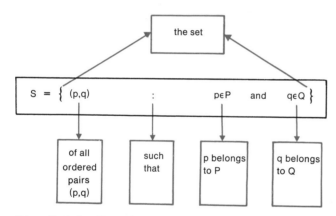

The set S is called the Cartesian product of P and Q and we denote it by

$$P \times Q$$

Definition 1
* * *

Notation 1

Discussion

The word "Cartesian" is derived from the surname Descartes. René Descartes was a famous seventeenth century French mathematician and philosopher who was the founder of *analytical geometry*, the application of algebra to geometry. His name was translated into Latin as "Renatus Cartesius", hence the adjective "Cartesian" which is perhaps best known when it appears in the phrase

"rectangular Cartesian co-ordinates"

describing a pair of axes used when drawing graphs in a plane, e.g.

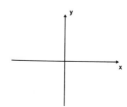

Example 1

Example 1

Let $P = \{K, Q, J\}$

and

$$Q = \left\{ \heartsuit, \clubsuit, \diamondsuit, \spadesuit \right\}$$

Then

$$P \times Q = \left\{ (K, \heartsuit), (Q, \heartsuit), (J, \heartsuit), (K, \clubsuit), (Q, \clubsuit), (J, \clubsuit), \right.$$
$$\left. (K, \diamondsuit), (Q, \diamondsuit), (J, \diamondsuit), (K, \spadesuit), (Q, \spadesuit), (J, \spadesuit) \right\} \quad \blacksquare$$

We can now consider mapping and function from a slightly different stand-point as follows:

> A subset of $P \times Q$ defines a mapping from P to Q if every element of P appears as the first term of at least one ordered pair of the subset.

Definition 2
* * *

> A subset of $P \times Q$ defines a function from P to Q if each element of P appears as the first term of an ordered pair of the subset once and once only.

Definition 3
* * *

(Note that the codomain Q is not necessarily defined by the subset of $P \times Q$ in either case, because there is not a requirement that every element of the codomain should appear as the second term of at least one ordered pair of the subset. Each element of the domain and its image is specified, however, and so the set of images of the elements of P is defined, and it is this set which is of importance.)

Example 2

Example 2

Probably the most frequently occurring collection of functions is the set of functions whose domain and codomain are subsets of the set of real numbers, R. Familiar examples are:

$$x \longmapsto a_1 x + a_0 \quad (x \in R) \quad \text{where } a_0, a_1 \in R$$
$$x \longmapsto \sin x \quad (x \in R)$$
$$x \longmapsto \log x \quad (x \in R^+)$$

(See RB11)

Each function of this kind can be identified with some particular subset of $R \times R$. Using the usual Cartesian co-ordinate system which we use for drawing graphs, the set $R \times R$ can be represented by the set of all points in a plane. Any subset of $R \times R$ then corresponds to a set of points in the plane.

Thus the subset of $R \times R$ with which we identify, for example, the function $x \longmapsto \sin x$, is represented by

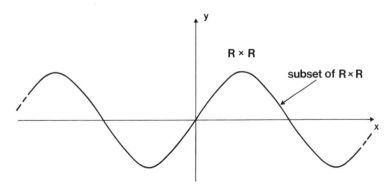

(continued on page 5)

Solution 1

Solution 1

(i), (iii), and (iv) define mappings; (ii) does not, because no images are assigned to the elements b and c.

The mappings (i) and (iv) define functions.

The mapping (iii) does not define a function because, for instance, the element a does not have a unique element as its image. ∎

(*continued from page 3*)

Some other possible subsets of $R \times R$ are represented by:

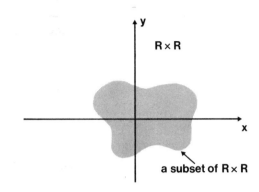

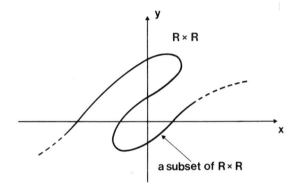

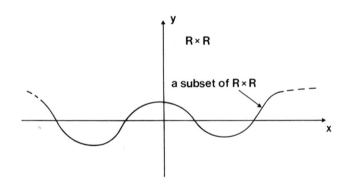

(The dotted ends of the curves are intended to mean that the curves extend indefinitely in the final direction indicated.) ■

Exercise 2

Why do *neither* of the first two of the three subsets of $R \times R$ depicted immediately above define a function $f : R \longrightarrow R$? ■

Solution 2 **Solution 2**

No *area* can define a function $R \longrightarrow R$. If the ordered pair (a, b) belongs to the area then there are other ordered pairs (a, c) with $c \neq b$ also belonging to the area, and a thus has more than one element in its image.

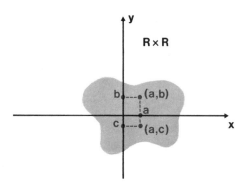

Similarly, in the case of the second subset illustrated, there will be elements such as a having more than one element in its image because of the way in which the curve "folds back" on itself.

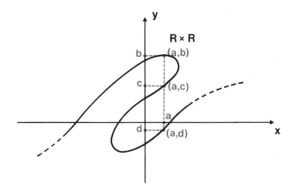

■

3.1.2 Binary Operations

We will begin this sub-section by investigating operations such as addition and multiplication, by which we combine two numbers to produce another number. Such operations are called *binary operations*.

The word "binary" arises because we combine *two* numbers. There are operations which act on one object and operations which operate on three (or more) objects. We shall discuss these other operations briefly in sub-section 3.1.5, but our main interest is in *binary* operations.

Example 1

Example 1

We are all familiar with $+$ representing the operation of addition in the set of real numbers R. For example, we have

$$3 + 5 = 8$$

We could rewrite this in our mapping notation as

$$+ : (3, 5) \longmapsto 8$$

This is not a particularly helpful way of writing down an addition sum, but it does illustrate the fact that the binary operation of addition on R *defines a function* with domain $R \times R$ and codomain R. (Note that this domain permits us to combine an element of R with itself.) ∎

As usual, we do not want to restrict ourselves to numbers, so we adopt the following definition of a binary operation:

> A binary operation, $\circ$, on a set A is a rule which assigns to *each* ordered pair $(a_1, a_2) \in A \times A$ a uniquely defined element b.

This is equivalent to saying that a binary operation on A is a function with domain $A \times A$, and codomain some set B.

We write

$$a_1 \circ a_2 = b$$

read
as
"circle"

If $a_1 \circ a_2$ belongs to A for all $a_1, a_2 \in A$, then we say that the binary operation is closed.

(More precisely, we should say that *A is closed for* $\circ$, since an operation cannot exist without a set. We shall, however, abbreviate.) A codomain of the function defined by a closed binary operation on A is therefore A itself.

Example 2

Example 2

Consider the binary operation of addition, $+$, on the set $\{0, 1, 2, 3, 4\}$. This is *not* closed because there are several pairs of elements of the set which can be added to give a result which is not a member of the original set, e.g. $2 + 4$. We can, however, devise a special kind of "addition" which will be a closed binary operation. One way of doing this is to add first, and then take the remainder on division by 5.

We shall now find that we always end up with an element of our set. Using the symbol $\oplus_5$ to denote this special sort of addition, we have, for example,

$$2 \oplus_5 4 = 1$$

$$3 \oplus_5 4 = 2$$

$$4 \oplus_5 4 = 3$$

Thus, "$\oplus_5$" is a closed binary operation on the set $\{0, 1, 2, 3, 4\}$, but "$+$" is not. ∎

We shall now look at another example in order to bring out a further property possessed by certain binary operations.

Example 3

Example 3

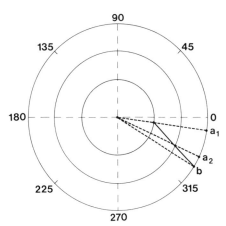

In this example the set A is

$$\{a : a \in R \text{ and } 0 \leqslant a < 360\}$$

We illustrate this set as the set of all points on the outer circle of our diagram, and we read off the corresponding numerical value by using the outside scale, as when reading degrees using a protractor. We now give a rule which enables us to combine two elements of A by an operation ∘ as follows:

> Take the point where the radius corresponding to a_1 cuts the inner circle and join it by a straight line to the point where the radius corresponding to a_2 cuts the middle circle. Continue this line to obtain the point b on the outer circle. The numerical value at b is defined to be $a_1 \circ a_2$.

For example, suppose that we take

$$a_1 = 45, \qquad a_2 = 225$$

The point where the radius at a_1 cuts the inner circle is the point P. Similarly, the point where the radius at a_2 cuts the middle circle is the point Q. If we now continue the line PQ to the outer circle we arrive at b, which in this case is a_2, thus:

$$45 \circ 225 = 225$$

If, however, we take

$$a_1 = 225$$
$$a_2 = 45$$

then we find that we obtain

$$225 \circ 45 = 45$$ ∎

So the *order* in which we take our pair of numbers is important, and for a binary operation $\circ$ on a set A, $a_1 \circ a_2$ *is not necessarily the same as* $a_2 \circ a_1$. If, as in the case of addition (and multiplication) on R, we have

$$a_1 \circ a_2 = a_2 \circ a_1$$

for *all* $a_1, a_2 \in A$, then the binary operation is said to be commutative. (This particular adjective is used because we may "commute" (i.e. interchange) the order of the elements.)

Definition 3
* * *

The following exercises are intended to make you familiar with the idea of a "binary operation".

Exercise 1

Exercise 1
(5 minutes)

(i) If A is the set of two numbers $\{0, 1\}$, is the operation of addition a closed binary operation on A?

(ii) We were careful to say that a binary operation defines a *function*. Why is it misleading, although not inaccurate, to say that a binary operation defines a mapping?

(iii) If A is a complete set of dominoes and we define the operation $\circ$, so that for example:

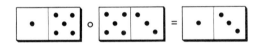

(we join pieces having a number in common just as in a normal game of dominoes), is $\circ$ a binary operation on the complete set of dominoes? ∎

Exercise 2

Exercise 2
(3 minutes)

In each of the following cases determine whether or not the binary operation $\circ$ on the set A is *closed*.

(i) $a_1 \circ a_2$ is $a_1 + a_2$;
A is the set of all real numbers, R. YES/NO

(ii) $a_1 \circ a_2$ is $a_1 - a_2$;
A is the set of positive integers, Z^+. YES/NO

(iii) $a_1 \circ a_2$ is $a_1 \div a_2$;
A is the set of integers, Z, excluding zero. YES/NO

(iv) $a_1 \circ a_2$ is the mid-point of the straight line joining a_1 and a_2;
A is the set of all points on a square piece of paper. YES/NO

(v) $a_1 \circ a_2$ is the mid-point of the straight line joining a_1 and a_2;
A is the set of all points on a square piece of paper with a circular hole cut out of it. YES/NO
∎

Exercise 3

Exercise 3
(2 minutes)

Classify the following list into two categories; those operations on A which are commutative, and those which are not commutative.

(i) $a_1 + a_2$;
(ii) $a_1 - a_2$; A is the set R
(iii) $\sin(a_1 + a_2)$;
(iv) $a_1 \div a_2$; A is the set R, excluding zero.
(v) The mid-point of the straight line joining points a_1 and a_2 on a square piece of paper; A is the set of all points on the paper. ∎

Solution 1
Solution 1

(i) NO, since $1 + 1 = 2$ is not a member of the set $\{0, 1\}$.

(ii) Because our definition of a binary operation $\circ$ states that $a_1 \circ a_2$ is a *uniquely defined element* (see p. 7). This is the very point which distinguishes the particular mappings which are functions.

(iii) NO, since the binary operation is *not defined* for some pairs of elements, e.g.:

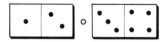

is not defined, and our definition of a binary operation on a set requires that any two elements of the set may be combined under $\circ$. ■

Solution 2
Solution 2

(i) YES. $a_1 + a_2$ is always a real number.

(ii) NO. Sometimes $a_1 - a_2$ may be a negative integer.

(iii) NO. $a_1 \div a_2$ need not be an integer.

(iv) YES. The mid-point for any two points is always on the paper.

(v) NO. The mid-point for some pairs of points may lie in the hole, which is not part of A. ■

Solution 3
Solution 3

Only in (ii) and (iv) are the binary operations *not* commutative. ■

3.1.3 Repeated Operations

Although by definition a binary operation ∘ on a set A combines only two elements, if the result of the operation is also an element of A (i.e. if ∘ is *closed* on A), then we can combine the result with a further element. Let us suppose then that for all $a_1, a_2 \in A$, we have an operation ∘ which gives us $a_1 \circ a_2$ in A, and let us now combine this result with a_3, where $a_3 \in A$. We denote the total result by

$$(a_1 \circ a_2) \circ a_3$$

The brackets enclose the elements that are combined first.

We have already seen that the order of the elements is important unless the operation is commutative, but does it matter if we combine a_1 and a_2 first, or a_2 and a_3 first? What we are asking in effect is:

$$does \quad (a_1 \circ a_2) \circ a_3 \quad equal \quad a_1 \circ (a_2 \circ a_3)?$$

The order of the terms in each expression is the same, but the way in which the terms are grouped is different.

Exercise 1

Of the following statements, which are true and which are false?

  (i) $x + (y + z) = (x + y) + z$, where $x, y, z \in R$.   TRUE/FALSE
  (ii) $x - (y - z) = (x - y) - z$, where $x, y, z \in R$.   TRUE/FALSE
  (iii) $(x^y)^z = x^{(y^z)}$, where $x, y, z \in Z^+$.   TRUE/FALSE

       (Here $x \circ y = x^y$, hence $(x \circ y) \circ z = (x^y)^z$, etc.)
  (iv) $x \div (y \div z) = (x \div y) \div z$, where $x, y, z \in R^+$.   TRUE/FALSE
  (v) $(x \times y) \times z = x \times (y \times z)$, where $x, y, z \in R$.   TRUE/FALSE
  (vi) $P \circ (Q \circ R) = (P \circ Q) \circ R$, where P, Q, R are points in a plane and $P \circ Q$ is the mid-point of the straight line joining P and Q.   TRUE/FALSE
  (vii) $x \circ (y \circ z) = (x \circ y) \circ z$, where $x, y, z \in R$, and ∘ is the operation of addition followed by rounding-off to three significant figures.   TRUE/FALSE
■

When the closed binary operation is such that

$$(a_1 \circ a_2) \circ a_3 = a_1 \circ (a_2 \circ a_3)$$

for *all* elements of A, we say that the operation is associative. This particular adjective is used to denote this property because we may "associate" either a_1 and a_2 (as on the left-hand side) or a_2 and a_3 (as on the right-hand side).

Exercise 2

Why was it necessary to require that the binary operation on A be *closed* when we discussed the idea of associativity?   ■

Solution 1

Solution 1

(i) TRUE.

(ii) FALSE, e.g. $2 - (3 - 4) \neq (2 - 3) - 4$.

(iii) FALSE, e.g. $(2^3)^2 = 64$, but $2^{(3^2)} = 512$.

(iv) FALSE, e.g. $12 \div (6 \div 2) \neq (12 \div 6) \div 2$.

(v) TRUE.

(iv) FALSE, e.g.:

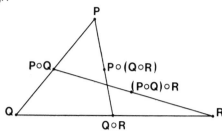

(vii) FALSE, e.g. $8.47 \circ (3.15 \circ 4.14) = 15.8$,

but $(8.47 \circ 3.15) \circ 4.14 = 15.7$. ■

Solution 2

Solution 2

Suppose that the operation $\circ$ is not closed. Then, for some $a_1, a_2 \in A$ we shall have an element $a_1 \circ a_2$, which will not belong to A.

If we now try to combine this $a_1 \circ a_2$ with a_3, we find that we are unable to do so because the operation $\circ$ is defined *on the set* A, so we are not entitled to try to use it to combine elements not belonging to A. ■

3.1.4 Two Binary Operations

Suppose now that we have a set with two closed binary operations. As an example we shall again take the set of all real numbers R, and we shall consider the operation of multiplication as well as addition. We start with three elements of R.

We have, for example,

$$2 \times (3 + 5)$$

We know that this is equal to

$$(2 \times 3) + (2 \times 5)$$

since in each case we obtain the number 16. In fact, no matter which three numbers we take, we always find that

$$x \times (y + z) = (x \times y) + (x \times z)$$

whenever $x, y, z \in R$.

This property of $\times$ and $+$ on R is a very useful one: for instance, it helps to simplify calculations, and without it the factorization of algebraic expressions would not be permissible. This leads us to ask of other pairs of binary operations whether they will obey a similar law. This is precisely the question asked in the next exercise for some particular pairs of binary operations.

Exercise 1

Of the following statements, which are true and which are false?

(i) $x + (y \times z) = (x + y) \times (x + z)$, where $x, y, z \in R$. TRUE/FALSE

(ii) $x + (y - z) = (x + y) - (x + z)$, where $x, y, z \in Z$. TRUE/FALSE

(iii) $x \times (y - z) = (x \times y) - (x \times z)$, where $x, y, z \in R$. TRUE/FALSE

(iv) $(y - z) \times x = (y \times x) - (z \times x)$, where $x, y, z \in R$. TRUE/FALSE

(v) $P \square (Q \circ R) = (P \square Q) \circ (P \square R)$, where P, Q, R are points in a plane, $Q \circ R$ is the mid-point of the straight line QR, and $P \square Q$ (read as P "square" Q) is the point on the line PQ extended so that the distance from P to Q is the same as the distance from Q to $P \square Q$. TRUE/FALSE

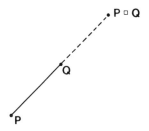

(vi) $(Q \circ R) \square P = (Q \square P) \circ (R \square P)$, where P, Q, R, $\circ$, $\square$ are the same as for (v). TRUE/FALSE

(vii) $(x + y) \div z = (x \div z) + (y \div z)$, where $x, y, z \in R^+$. TRUE/FALSE

(viii) $z \div (x + y) = (z \div x) + (z \div y)$, where $x, y, z \in R^+$. TRUE/FALSE

■

When two closed binary operations, $\square$ and $\circ$, on a set A have the property that

$$a_1 \square (a_2 \circ a_3) = (a_1 \square a_2) \circ (a_1 \square a_3)$$

for *all* elements of A, we say that the operation $\square$ is left-distributive over the operation $\circ$.

(*continued on page 14*)

Solution 1

   (i) FALSE, e.g. $2 + (3 \times 4) \neq (2 + 3) \times (2 + 4)$.

  (ii) FALSE, e.g. $2 + (3 - 4) \neq (2 + 3) - (2 + 4)$.

 (iii) TRUE.

 (iv) TRUE. Because multiplication is commutative, we can deduce (iv) from (iii). The order in which y and z appear has to be preserved in each case, however, because subtraction is not commutative.

  (v) TRUE, e.g.

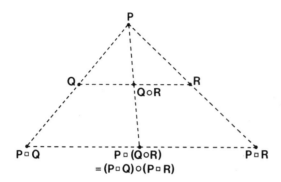

        The result can be easily proved by reference to "similar triangles".   (See RB6)

 (vi) TRUE. Although, because $\square$ is not commutative, we cannot deduce (vi) from (v), in the same way as we can deduce (iv) from (iii).

(vii) TRUE.

(viii) FALSE, e.g. $8 \div (1 + 3) \neq (8 \div 1) + (8 \div 3)$.   ■

(continued from page 13)

So, multiplication is left-distributive over addition on R. ("Left" is used because $\square$ stands on the left (once) before being distributed (twice) over ∘.)

Similarly $(a_1 \circ a_2) \square a_3 = (a_1 \square a_3) \circ (a_2 \square a_3)$

is a definition of right-distributivity of $\square$ over ∘.   Definition 2
                                                  ★ ★

If the operation $\square$ is commutative, then one can be inferred from the other as in (iii) and (iv) of Exercise 1.

On the other hand, parts (vii) and (viii) of this exercise show that division is right-distributive but not left-distributive over addition.

We shall now define the single term distributive to mean left- and right-distributive.   Definition 3
                                                  ★ ★ ★

3.1.5 *N*-ary Operations

In sub-section 3.1.2, we saw that a binary operation on *A* defines a function with domain $A \times A$ and vice versa. We ought not to be surprised at this very close relation between a binary operation and a function because, after all, the idea of a *rule* is present in both concepts.

We have so far concentrated our interest on *binary* operations because the idea of an operation as such comes to mind most naturally when we consider combining two elements of a given set. But the close connection between a binary operation on *A* and a function with domain $A \times A$ leads us to re-examine functions briefly.

Example 1

Example 1

Consider the function

$$x \longmapsto x^2 \quad (x \in R)$$

The rule which tells us how to obtain the image of any given element of *R* can be regarded as an *operation* on *R*. In this case the operation is

> square it

Because here we are operating on *only one* element of *R* at a time, we call such an operation a unary operation. The word "unary" (compare "unit") arises because we "operate on *one* element" at a time. ■

Example 1 illustrates a function $f : A \longrightarrow B$, where the image set is a subset of the domain *A*, and we can therefore interpret this function as a *closed* unary operation.

We can also ask ourselves about operations on a set which combine three or more elements to give one element of the same or a different set. Again there is the same close connection with the idea of a function, and we can construct a simple table to illustrate this.

Operation ∘ on a set *A* acts on:	Operation is called	Corresponding function
single element a_1	UNARY	$f : A \longrightarrow B$
ordered pair (a_1, a_2)	BINARY	$f : A \times A \longrightarrow B$
ordered triple (a_1, a_2, a_3)	TERNARY	$f : A \times A \times A \longrightarrow B$
. . . .	. . . .	. . . .
ordered *n*-tuple $(a_1, a_2, \ldots, a_n)$	N-ARY	$f : \underbrace{A \times A \times \cdots \times A}_{n \text{ times}} \longrightarrow B$

In the table we have introduced the notation $A \times A \times A$ to mean the set

$$\{(a_1, a_2, a_3) : a_1, a_2, a_3 \in A\}$$

i.e. the set of all ordered triples that can be formed from elements of *A*. This is the notation which is usual in the mathematical literature. The notation is extended in the obvious way as we go down the table.

Whether we choose to talk about an operation or its corresponding function is purely a matter of context. Sometimes it is more natural to speak of such and such an operation, sometimes of such and such a function.

Example 2

Example 2

Consider the function

$$(x, y, z) \longmapsto xyz \quad ((x, y, z) \in R \times R \times R)$$

If we consider this as an *operation on R*, then it is a *ternary* operation, since it combines by multiplication three elements of R. However, we can also consider it as an *operation on $R \times R \times R$*, in which case it is a *unary* operation, since it operates on only one element of $R \times R \times R$ at a time. ∎

We have singled out the *binary* operation for special emphasis because, as we have already remarked, this is the way in which the idea of an operation most naturally arises. We shall, however, use the idea of a unary operation also, in the early part of the next section.

Exercise 1

How would you define the set A so that the function

$$(x, y) \longmapsto x^3 y^2 \quad ((x, y) \in R \times R)$$

corresponds to

 (i) a binary
(ii) a unary

operation on A?

Which, if either, of the operations would be closed?   ■

17

Solution 1

(i) Let A be the set R.

The function is then $A \times A \longrightarrow A$, and since the set of images is A, the operation is a *closed* binary operation on A.

(ii) Let A be the set $R \times R$.

The function is then $A \longrightarrow R$. Now the elements of A are all ordered pairs, but the elements of R are not. So R is not a subset of A, and hence the operation is a unary operation but *not* a closed unary operation.

■

3.1.6 Summary

In this part of the unit, we have shown how the concepts of function and operation are closely connected — indeed, in one sense, almost synonymous.

We have also defined a binary (and *n*-ary) operation, and the terms

closed, commutative, associative, distributive.

These properties of an operation are so fundamental, when present, that you will find in subsequent units that among the first questions we ask of any new operation is: "Does it possess any or all of these properties?"

3.2 MORPHISMS

3.2.0 Introduction

In this section we are going to discuss a particularly important mathematical concept called a morphism which is closely related to the concept of a *mathematical model*. (You may find it useful at this stage to re-read the introduction on p. x.)

Mathematics today has applications in all sorts of ways which were undreamt of a few decades ago. We are able to apply mathematics in such varied fields of study as the pure and applied sciences, the social sciences, commerce, architecture, music, etc., because situations in the physical world around us can be translated into mathematics, or, to say the same thing in different words, because mathematics can *model* situations in the physical world.

The idea of a *mathematical model* is fundamental to the proper understanding of this section. The value of mathematical models lies in the fact that with pencil and paper (and possibly also a computer) all kinds of situations can be investigated, and designs worked out, which would otherwise be unacceptably expensive in terms of time, space and materials.

But mathematics provides us also with many useful opportunities of *modelling mathematics*. That is to say, having set up a mathematical problem in one particular way, we may find ourselves wanting to tackle the problem from an entirely different stand-point, because our initial statement of the problem in mathematical terms raises difficulties of understanding or of calculation. It is then that we seek an alternative approach, i.e. we look for a mathematical model of the mathematics.

We shall begin by considering operations, then we shall use the close link between functions and operations, established earlier in the unit, to develop our ideas in a more useful and general form.

3.2.1 How Morphisms Arise

Let us suppose that we have a set with a *closed* binary operation and a *closed* unary operation. As our specific example, we shall consider the set R together with the binary operation of addition and the unary operation defined by the rule

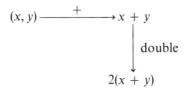

Now we know that

$$2(x + y) = 2x + 2y \quad (x, y \in R)$$

Equation (1)

i.e. multiplication by 2 is distributive over addition. The left-hand side of our expression represents performing the binary operation first and then the unary operation, and we can represent this diagrammatically. We start with two elements of R, perform an addition, and obtain a single element of R, and we represent this by the diagram:

$$(x, y) \xrightarrow{\ +\ } x + y$$

We now perform the unary operation and obtain another single element of R, and we represent the whole process by

$$(x, y) \xrightarrow{\ +\ } x + y$$
$$\downarrow \text{double}$$
$$2(x + y)$$

The right-hand side of Equation (1) represents our performing the unary operation first, and this is performed upon each of the two elements of R separately, so we have

$$(x, y)$$
$$\text{double} \downarrow$$
$$(2x, 2y)$$

Now, performing the binary operation, we have

$$(x, y)$$
$$\text{double} \downarrow$$
$$(2x, 2y) \xrightarrow{\ +\ } 2x + 2y$$

and *because of the distributivity of multiplication over addition* we arrive at the same result as before, namely $2x + 2y = 2(x + y)$. We can thus put the diagrams representing the left- and right-hand sides of our expression together to give us:

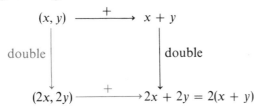

When we have a diagram, such as this, which permits alternative paths from the same starting point to the same finishing point, we call it a commutative diagram. We use the word "commutative" because the order in which we perform the binary and unary operations is different in the two possible paths, and we can thus loosely think of the operations being commutative.

Definition 1
* * *

$$\xrightarrow{\quad +\quad} \xrightarrow{\quad \text{double} \quad} = \xrightarrow{\quad \text{double} \quad} \xrightarrow{\quad +\quad}$$

Exercise 1

Exercise 1
(3 minutes)

Can we draw a commutative diagram for the set R with the operations

(i) $\times$ and $\boxed{\text{square it}}$?   YES/NO

(ii) $+$ and $\boxed{\text{square it}}$?   YES/NO

If your answer is YES, draw the corresponding commutative diagram. ■

So far, we have taken as our starting point one set and two *closed* operations, one a binary operation and the other a unary operation. Suppose now that we drop the closure restriction on the unary operation, and, looking back to section 3.1.5, recall that a unary operation is merely another way of looking at a *function*

Discussion

$$f : A \longrightarrow B$$

This means that we take up a somewhat more general point of view, starting with a set A with closed binary operation $\circ$, and also a function

$$f : A \longmapsto B = f(A)$$

Let us first see how far we can get with our diagram. We will start with an ordered pair of elements from our set as we did before, and we shall continue to use a horizontal arrow to depict the binary operation and a vertical arrow to depict the function.

This gives:

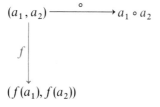

Since the binary operation $\circ$ is closed, we have $a_1 \circ a_2 \in A$, and we can now draw a vertical arrow (depicting the function) on the right-hand side of the diagram.

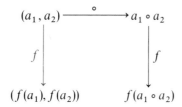

Having obtained three sides of a commutative diagram, our problem now is what to do about the final side. Remembering that the missing arrow should represent the combination of $f(a_1)$ and $f(a_2)$ by some binary operation, we ask ourselves the question:

> Is there a binary operation, say $\square$, on $f(A)$ such that
> $$f(a_1) \square f(a_2) = f(a_1 \circ a_2)$$
> for all $a_1, a_2 \in A$?

Our first reaction to this question will probably be to see if the binary operation $\circ$, defined on A, will do what we want. But we must remember that unless the image set $f(A)$ is a subset of A, we are not entitled to combine elements of $f(A)$ using $\circ$. In certain circumstances, as we shall see, it may be possible to *extend* our original definition of $\circ$ so that we can combine elements of $f(A)$ using $\circ$ even though $f(A)$ is not a subset of A. We now look at three particular examples.

Example 1

Example 1

Consider the closed binary operation of addition on R and the function (unary operation):

$$f : x \longmapsto |x| \quad (x \in R)$$

the modulus function which we have already met in previous units, for which

$$f(x) = \quad x \quad \text{if } x \geqslant 0$$
$$f(x) = -x \quad \text{if } x < 0$$

In this case, the set of all images is the set R_0^+ (the positive real numbers with zero) and, as this is a subset of R, it is clear that the operation of addition defined on R can be performed on the images in just the same way as it can be performed on the elements of R.

Let us now see how far we can get with a diagram. For $x, y \in R$, we have:

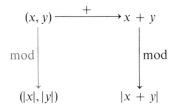

We are allowed to try to use "$+$" to complete the diagram since

$$|x| + |y|$$

is defined. Unfortunately, however, it is not generally true that

$$|x| + |y| = |x + y| \quad (x, y \in R)$$

For instance, for $x = -2$ and $y = 2$, we have $|x| + |y| = 4$ and $|x + y| = 0$.

So, although we can combine $|x|$ and $|y|$ using "$+$", this will not bring us to the same result as that which we obtained when we performed the addition first, and performed the modulus mapping second. Thus, we cannot in this case use $+$ for $\square$. ∎

(continued on page 22)

Solution 1

Solution 1

(i) YES,

$$(x \times y)^2 = x^2 \times y^2 \quad (x, y \in R)$$

(ii) NO,

$$(x + y)^2 \neq x^2 + y^2 \quad (x, y \in R)$$

For (i) we have the commutative diagram

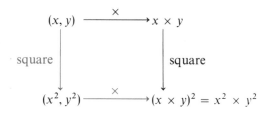

(*continued from page 21*)

Example 2

Example 2

Consider the closed binary operation of addition on R^+ and the function

$$f : x \longmapsto -\sqrt{x} \quad (x \in R^+)$$

We have immediately for $x, y \in R^+$:

$$
\begin{array}{ccc}
(x, y) & \xrightarrow{\ +\ } & x + y \\
\ \downarrow{\scriptstyle -\sqrt{\ }} & & \ \downarrow{\scriptstyle -\sqrt{\ }} \\
(-\sqrt{x}, -\sqrt{y}) & & -\sqrt{(x + y)}
\end{array}
$$

Now, the function is $R^+ \longmapsto R^-$ (the set of negative real numbers) and, since R^- is not a subset of R^+ (the set on which we have defined our original binary operation), we cannot immediately combine elements of the image set using "$+$". Addition is, however, definable on all the real numbers, and so it is readily interpreted on R^-. Once we have so extended the definition of the binary operation "$+$", we can see if it can be used to complete the diagram. Unfortunately, we are again in a position exactly similar to that of the previous example, since

$$(-\sqrt{x}) + (-\sqrt{y}) \neq -\sqrt{(x + y)}$$

For example, for $x = 9$ and $y = 16$, we have

$$(-\sqrt{x}) + (-\sqrt{y}) = -7 \quad \text{and} \quad -\sqrt{(x + y)} = 5$$

So, again, we cannot use $+$ for $\square$. ∎

Example 3

Example 3

Consider the closed binary operation of multiplication on R and the function

$$f : x \longmapsto x^n \quad (x \in R)$$

(where n is an integer).

We have immediately for $x, y \in R$:

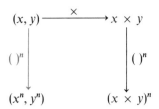

Since our original binary operation " $\times$ " is defined on the image set, and since, further,

$$x^n \times y^n = (x \times y)^n \quad (x, y \in R)$$

we can use $\times$ to complete our commutative diagram and obtain:

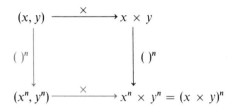

■

Exercise 2

Exercise 2
(5 minutes)

For each of the given sets A, binary operations $\circ$ on A, and functions f, comment on the use of $\circ$ on the image set and state, when appropriate, if the commutative diagram can be completed.

Draw the completed diagram where possible.

(i) set A: R (excluding zero)
    binary operation $\circ$: $\times$
    function f: $x \longmapsto \dfrac{1}{x}$ $(x \in A)$

(ii) set A: R^+
    binary operation $\circ$: $+$
    function f: $x \longmapsto \dfrac{1}{+\sqrt{x}}$ $(x \in A)$

(iii) set A: Z^+ (the set of positive integers)
    binary operation $\circ$: $\times$
    function f: $\left.\begin{array}{l} x \longmapsto 0, \text{ when } x \text{ is even} \\ x \longmapsto 1, \text{ when } x \text{ is odd} \end{array}\right\}$ $(x \in A)$

(iv) set A: R (excluding zero)
    binary operation $\circ$: $\div$
    function f: $x \longmapsto 1 - x$ $(x \in A)$ ■

What we have been considering so far is a special case of the more general problem we posed originally on page 21:

Main Text
* * *

> Is there a binary operation $\square$ on $f(A)$ such that
>
> $$f(a_1) \square f(a_2) = f(a_1 \circ a_2)$$
>
> for all $a_1, a_2 \in A$?

(continued on page 24)

Solution 2 **Solution 2**

(i) The elements of the image set may be combined using "$\times$".
YES, a commutative diagram can then be formed.

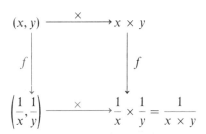

(ii) The elements of the image set may be combined using "$+$".
NO, a commutative diagram cannot be formed, e.g.

$$\frac{1}{+\sqrt{4}} + \frac{1}{+\sqrt{9}} \neq \frac{1}{+\sqrt{(4+9)}}$$

(iii) The binary operation "$\times$" is defined on Z^+ and zero is not a member of this set. The operation must therefore first be extended to the set of images $\{0, 1\}$. We illustrate the diagram for one of the cases:

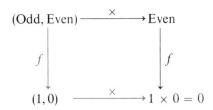

(iv) The function maps R (excluding zero) to R (excluding 1), and division is not defined on any subset of R which includes zero. We thus cannot use $\div$ to combine elements of the image set. ∎

(continued from page 23)

Example 4 **Example 4**

Consider

$$f : x \longmapsto \log x \quad (x \in R^+)$$

(See RB11)

and the closed binary operation of multiplication. We have:

$$
\begin{array}{ccc}
(x, y) & \xrightarrow{\;\times\;} & x \times y \\[2pt]
\downarrow{\scriptstyle \log} & & \downarrow{\scriptstyle \log} \\[2pt]
(\log x, \log y) & \xrightarrow{\;\square\,?\;} & \log(x \times y)
\end{array}
$$

Because of the properties of the function $x \longmapsto \log x$, $(x \in R^+)$, we know that

$$\log(x \times y) = \log x + \log y$$

24

(It is this particular property that enables us to use logarithms for calculating products.) So we *can* complete our diagram using the binary operation of *addition* on the bottom line to give us:

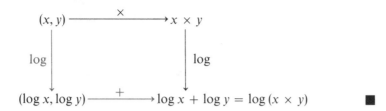

More generally, we would have:

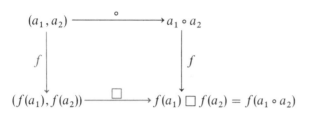

Whenever we can "complete the rectangle" in this way using either the same or a different binary operation in the image set, the function f is called a morphism from the set A with binary operation $\circ$, written $(A, \circ)$, to the set $f(A)$ with binary operation $\square$, written $(f(A), \square)$.*

Definition 2
* * *

We write

Notation 1
* * *

$$f:(A, \circ)\longmapsto(f(A), \square)$$

In the simplest of cases $f(A)$ is a subset of A and $\square$ is the same as $\circ$, but in many of the examples which are of use in mathematical situations, such as the logarithm example, we have a *modelling* of one set with a binary operation by another set with a different binary operation.

We can, if we like, think of the function $f:A\longmapsto f(A)$ providing us with an "image" of the binary operation defined on A, just as it provides us with images of the elements of A and of A itself. Thus, in our logarithm example, we can think of addition on R as being the image of multiplication on R^2, and we could write $f(\times) = +$ to express this.

Discussion
* *

The importance of morphisms lies in their modelling property. Thus, we may have a physical situation with perhaps some mechanical or electrical operation which we model by selecting a suitable mathematical set and operation. We can then draw the diagram as:

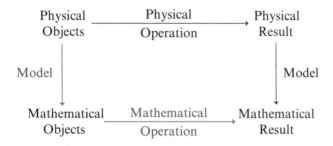

(A simple example of this was given in the introduction on page x.)

---

* Many authors define a morphism f from $(A, \circ)$ to $(B, \square)$, where B is the codomain but not necessarily the image set of A under f. There is no advantage to us at this stage in this slightly more general definition.

In practice, the process used corresponds to a modified commutative diagram:

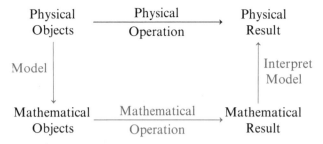

In other words, the usefulness of the model will depend very largely upon whether or not we can go from the mathematical result to the physical result. That is, the usefulness depends on our being able to reverse the right-hand arrow, and on the sort of interpretation which we can put on the mathematical results when we translate them back into the physical situation. The reversal of the arrow corresponds to the finding of the reverse mapping of $f : A \longmapsto B$, i.e. $g : B \longmapsto A$, *and this is not necessarily a function.*

In the case of modelling a physical situation, we have the additional problems associated with re-interpreting an idealized mathematical model, and we must always remember that our mathematical model may well represent only certain features of the physical situation, and so our mathematical result will at best be a good *approximation* to the physical result. We shall not enquire further in this text into the mathematical modelling of physical situations, except for the one example of dimensional analysis at the end.

(The word "morphism" is derived from the Greek word $\mu o \rho \phi \acute{\eta}$ meaning "form"; compare "metamorphosis", meaning "changing of form". It is used here because a morphism is a "form-preserving" or "structure-preserving" function.)

Exercise 3

If f is a morphism $f : (A, \circ) \longmapsto (f(A), \square)$, is the reverse mapping $g : (f(A), \square) \longmapsto (A, \circ)$ necessarily a morphism? ∎

Exercise 3
(2 minutes)

We have just seen that in the *many–one* case, the reverse of a morphism is not a morphism. Suppose, however, that the morphism

$$f : (A, \circ) \longmapsto (f(A), \square)$$

is *one–one*. In this case, the reverse mapping

$$g : (f(A), \square) \longmapsto (A, \circ)$$

is one–one and the inverse function of f. Let us start with two elements of B, and see how far we can get with a commutative diagram. For $b_1, b_2 \in f(A)$, we have

Discussion

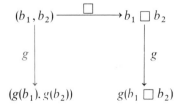

Can we now complete the diagram by using the binary operation "$\circ$", i.e. does

$$g(b_1) \circ g(b_2) = g(b_1 \square b_2)?$$

Recalling one of Polya's suggestions,* *Polya* xvii, under the heading DEVISING A PLAN, we should ask ourselves at this point:

"Did we use all the data?

Did we use the whole condition?

Have we taken into account all essential notions involved in the problem?"

This should bring us to realize that we have not used the obvious piece of information that f is a one–one morphism and that g is the inverse function of f. We can introduce this into the argument by supposing that

$$\left.\begin{array}{ll} f(a_1) = b_1 & \text{i.e. that } g(b_1) = a_1 \\ f(a_2) = b_2 & \text{i.e. that } g(b_2) = a_2 \end{array}\right\} \begin{array}{l} \text{because} \\ f \text{ is} \\ \text{one–one} \end{array}$$

Then $g(b_1) \circ g(b_2) = a_1 \circ a_2$, and, using the fact that f is a morphism, we have

$$f(a_1 \circ a_2) = f(a_1) \,\square\, f(a_2)$$
$$= b_1 \,\square\, b_2$$

Again, since f is one–one and g is its inverse it follows that

$$a_1 \circ a_2 = g(b_1 \,\square\, b_2)$$

whence

$$g(b_1) \circ g(b_2) = g(b_1 \,\square\, b_2)$$

and we can therefore complete our diagram using "$\circ$". Thus, *the inverse of a one–one morphism is a morphism.*

If you found this discussion difficult, then it may be worth spending some time understanding it and then writing it out in your own words. It is typical of the kind of formal argument common in modern algebra. The problem does not lie in the technical detail, but rather in mastering and ordering the facts into a coherent proof.

We shall now digress somewhat from our main story-line and look briefly at two kinds of morphism.

* G. Polya, *How to Solve It*, Open University ed. (Doubleday Anchor Books, 1970). This book is the set book for the Mathematics Foundation Course; it is referred to in the text as *Polya*.

Solution 3

NO.

If the function f is *many–one*, then the reverse mapping g is *one–many* and *not a function*. Since a morphism, by definition, is a function (with special properties), g cannot be a morphism.

3.2.2 Kinds of Morphism

In the last sub-section we encountered two particular morphisms, namely

$$\log:(R^+, \times)\longmapsto(R, +)$$

and

$$f:(Z^+, \times)\longmapsto(\{0, 1\}, \times)$$

where

$$\begin{rcases} x\longmapsto 0 \quad (x\text{ even}) \\ x\longmapsto 1 \quad (x\text{ odd}) \end{rcases} (x \in Z^+).$$

Notice that the former is *one–one* while the latter is *many–one*.

When the function is *one–one* the morphism is called an isomorphism. When the function is *many–one* the morphism is called a homomorphism. Thus, the function $x\longmapsto\log x$ $(x \in R^+)$ is an isomorphism of $(R^+, \times)$ to $(R, +)$. On the other hand, the function

$$\begin{rcases} x\longmapsto 0 \quad (x\text{ even}) \\ x\longmapsto 1 \quad (x\text{ odd}) \end{rcases} (x \in Z^+).$$

is a homomorphism of $(Z^+, \times)$ to $(\{0, 1\}, \times)$.

We can now restate our solution to Exercise 3.2.1.3 and the subsequent discussion as follows:

> *The reverse of a homomorphism is not a morphism;*
> *the inverse of an isomorphism is an isomorphism.*

Exercise 1

Classify each of the following morphisms as a *homomorphism* or as an *isomorphism*.

(i) $f:(R, \times)\longmapsto(R_0^+, \times)$

where $f:x\longmapsto|x|$.

(ii) $f:(A, \circ)\longmapsto(A, \circ)$

where $f:a\longmapsto a$.

(iii) $f:(Z^+, +)\longmapsto(\{0, 1, 2\}, \oplus_3)$

where $f:x\longmapsto x_3$, where x_3 is the remainder after division of x by 3, and $\oplus_3$ is a special kind of "addition", namely *add and then take the remainder on division by three*. (Compare with Example 3.1.2.2.)

We return now to our logarithm example,

$$\log : (R^+, \times) \longmapsto (R, +)$$

which we have seen to be an *isomorphism*. Because f is *one–one*, we are able to invert the right-hand arrow of the appropriate commutative diagram and obtain each image $g(\log x + \log y)$ uniquely. We call g the anti-logarithm, and we thus have as our diagram:

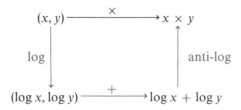

We are able in this case to go from (x, y) to $x \times y$ without carrying out the operation of multiplication explicitly, by following the process represented by the other three sides of our rectangle, each one giving us a unique result, i.e. we perform

$$\xrightarrow{\quad f \quad} \xrightarrow{\quad + \quad} \xrightarrow{\quad g \quad}$$

and it is this uniqueness of our result that enables us to multiply numbers using the addition of logarithms.

In practice, we can do a similar rearrangement of the commutative diagram when the morphism f is a homomorphism; only it is not just as simple as reversing the right-hand arrow, because, since f is many–one, when we reverse the arrow (i.e. use the reverse mapping), we are likely to get more than one element in the image at the top right. This difficulty is usually resolved by external considerations. For example, suppose we use logarithms recording only the decimal part (much in the way one uses a slide rule), e.g. for the image of 20 we record log 2. Then instead of an isomorphism we have a homomorphism, but we can still proceed this far:

$$(28, 39) \xrightarrow{\quad \times \quad} \text{approx. } 30 \times 40 = 1200$$

$$\downarrow \log$$

$$(\log 2.8, \log 3.9) \xrightarrow{\quad + \quad} \log 2.8 + \log 3.9$$

and the anti-log of $(\log 2.8 + \log 3.9)$ will give the right answer except for the position of the decimal point, and this is settled by our approximate value of the answer.

In our logarithm example, we were in a situation where we, as it were "happened to know" that addition was the binary operation defined on the image set which would enable us to complete our commutative diagram. We were not, however, in a situation where we had any room to manoeuvre; *no other operation on the image set would do*. Thus, once the function together with its domain and the binary operation on that domain are prescribed, the binary operation on the image set is also determined, and for this reason we call it the induced binary operation. In our next sub-section we shall take up this point and consider the conditions in which the induced binary operation may exist, and look at one or two specific examples where, having assured ourselves of its existence, we then try to find out what the operation is.

Solution 1 **Solution 1**

(i) Homomorphism; e.g.

$$-2 \longmapsto 2$$

and

$$2 \longmapsto 2$$

i.e. the function is many–one.

(ii) Isomorphism. If $a \neq b$, then $f(a) \neq f(b)$, i.e. the function is one–one.

(iii) Homomorphism; e.g.

$$1 \longmapsto 1$$

$$4 \longmapsto 1$$

$$7 \longmapsto 1, \text{ etc.}$$

i.e. the function is many–one. ■

3.2.3   Looking for Morphisms

In sub-section 3.2.1 we concerned ourselves with the question:

> Is there a binary operation $\square$ on the set $f(A)$ such that
>
> $$f(a_1) \square f(a_2) = f(a_1 \circ a_2)$$
>
> for all $a_1, a_2 \in A$?

where we had taken as our starting point a set A with a closed binary operation $\circ$, and a function $f: A \longmapsto f(A)$. So far, any attempt to answer this question has been entirely a "hit or miss" affair. We shall now try to look at the problem more systematically and ask ourselves if there is any condition which we can state *solely in terms of our set A, a closed binary operation $\circ$ and function f*, which will give us a guarantee of the existence of an induced operation $\square$ on $f(A)$.

Exercise 1

Following Polya's lead let us list what we know:

List 1

$$A, \quad \circ, \quad f$$

The list of what we would like to find (define) contains just one element:

List 2

$$\square$$

Is there anything wrong with defining $\square$ on the set $f(A)$ by

$$f(a_1) \square f(a_2) = f(a_1 \circ a_2)?$$

(If you would like to make use of it, a hint follows.) ■

HINT:

Try a few particular cases, (*Polya* xvi–xvii), e.g.

(i) $A = R$; $\circ$ is $+$; $f = [x \longmapsto \sin x, \quad (x \in R)]$;

(ii) $A = R$; $\circ$ is $\times$; $f = [x \longmapsto x^2, \quad (x \in R)]$;

(iii) $A = R$; $\circ$ is $+$; $f = [x \longmapsto x^2, \quad (x \in R)]$;

(iv) $A = R$; $\circ$ is $+$; $f = [x \longmapsto x^3, \quad (x \in R)]$.

Discussion of hint for the solution of Exercise 1

(i) Let us make a choice for a_1 and a_2, say

$$a_1 = \pi, \qquad a_2 = \frac{3\pi}{4}$$

$$\sin a_1 = 0, \qquad \sin a_2 = \frac{1}{\sqrt{2}}$$

$$\sin (a_1 + a_2) = \sin \frac{7\pi}{4} = -\frac{1}{\sqrt{2}}$$

Therefore, assuming that we have defined $\square$ as suggested above,

$$0 \;\square\; \frac{1}{\sqrt{2}} = -\frac{1}{\sqrt{2}}$$

But the sine mapping is a many–one mapping, and there are other elements of A which map to 0 and $\dfrac{1}{\sqrt{2}}$: for instance 2π maps to 0 and $\dfrac{\pi}{4}$ maps to $\dfrac{1}{\sqrt{2}}$; what happens if we set

$$a_1 = 2\pi, \qquad a_2 = \frac{\pi}{4}?$$

Verify that we now get $0 \;\square\; \dfrac{1}{\sqrt{2}} = \dfrac{1}{\sqrt{2}}$.

This will not do; for a binary operation, the answer must be *unique*.

Can you now answer the question in the exercise?

(ii) In this case there will always be two and only two (except for 0) numbers having one and the same given image. Thus

$$f(x) = f(-x) = x^2$$

$$f(y) = f(-y) = y^2$$

Let $a_1 = 2$ and $a_2 = 3$, then $4 \;\square\; 9 = f(2 \times 3) = 36$.

Let $a_1 = -2$ and $a_2 = 3$, then $4 \;\square\; 9 = f(-2 \times 3) = 36$.

However you choose a_1 and a_2 mapping to 4 and 9, respectively, you will find

$$4 \;\square\; 9 = 36$$

So, in this case, the definition of $\square$ in the exercise *seems* a good one.

Can you now answer the question in the exercise?

(iii) $a_1 = 2$, $a_2 = 3$, then $4 \;\square\; 9 = f(2 + 3) = 25$. $a_1 = -2$, $a_2 = 3$, then $4 \;\square\; 9 = f(-2 + 3) = 1$. So the definition of $\square$ is answered as in (i).

Can you now answer the question in the exercise?

(iv) $a_1 = 2$, $a_2 = 3$, then $8 \;\square\; 27 = f(2 + 3) = 125$, and there are no other numbers in R which map to 8 or 27 under this mapping. Since the function f is one–one in this case we will always get a unique answer for $x^3 \;\square\; y^3$, i.e. $(x + y)^3$.

Can you now answer the question in the exercise?

Solution 1

Following on from the discussion of the hints we argue as follows:

From (i) it appears that where f is many–one we are likely to run into trouble. We require $\square$ to be a binary operation, i.e. to give a unique answer to the combination of two elements of the image set $f(A)$. Since $f(a_1)$ and $f(a_2)$, considered as elements of $f(A)$, can arise from elements in A other than a_1 and a_2, we are in danger, as (i) illustrates, of not getting the unique answer we require.

In order that we should not be tempted to say that the definition of $\square$ only works when f is one–one, we have (ii), where f is many–one but the definition works. In (ii), of course, we recognize $\square$ as $\times$. In (iii) again the definition does not work; f is many–one. Just in case we should be tempted to say that the definition for $\square$ only works when there is an obvious known interpretation of $\square$, we inserted (iv), where the definition works but $\square$ is a little unusual. In this last case f is one–one, and our definition is always satisfactory for one–one functions. That is, given A, $\circ$ and a one–one function f, we can always complete the commutative diagram:

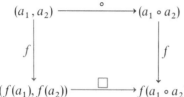

where $\square$ is *defined* by

$$f(a_1) \,\square\, f(a_2) = f(a_1 \circ a_2)$$

for all $a_1, a_2 \in A$.

That is, there is always a closed binary operation on $f(A)$ which makes f into an isomorphism.

The problem is more difficult when f is many–one. In the following text we deal with this. (We realize that this exercise was somewhat "tougher" and more abstract than most of the earlier exercises. It was for this reason we decided to give you the hint to try some particular cases. If you have found it difficult, despite the help which we tried to give you, then we suggest that you "leave it aside" for the moment, and come back to it after reading through the remainder of the text material.) ∎

Following on the experience we have gained in discussing Exercise 1, we introduce the following definition:

> A function f with domain A and a binary operation $\circ$ on A are compatible if whenever
>
> $$f(a_1) = f(a_2)$$
>
> and
>
> $$f(a_3) = f(a_4)$$
>
> then
>
> $$f(a_1 \circ a_3) = f(a_2 \circ a_4)$$
>
> $a_1, a_2, a_3, a_4 \in A$.

(We shall see a little later that compatibility is the condition required to be able to define the induced binary operation $\square$ on $f(A)$.)

Example 1

Example 1

      Set A: R
      Binary operation $\circ$: $+$
      Function f: $x \longmapsto \sin x$ $(x \in A)$

Let

$$a_1 = 0$$

$$a_2 = \pi$$

$$a_3 = a_4 = \frac{\pi}{4}$$

Then

$$f(a_1) = \sin 0 = 0$$

$$f(a_2) = \sin \pi = 0 = f(a_1)$$

$$f(a_3) = f(a_4) = \sin \frac{\pi}{4} = \frac{1}{\sqrt{2}}$$

However,

$$f(a_1 \circ a_3) = \sin\left(0 + \frac{\pi}{4}\right)$$

$$\neq f(a_2 \circ a_4) = \sin\left(\pi + \frac{\pi}{4}\right)$$

So the function $x \longmapsto \sin x$ $(x \in R)$ and the binary operation of addition are *not* compatible.   ■

Example 2

Example 2

      Set A: R
      Binary Operation $\circ$: $\times$
      Function f: $x \longmapsto x^2$ $(x \in A)$

In this case, there will always be two and only two numbers having one and the same given image. Thus,

$$f(x) = f(-x) = x^2$$

$$f(y) = f(-y) = y^2$$

and

$$f(x \times y) = f(x \times (-y)) = f((-x) \times y) = f((-x) \times (-y))$$

$$= x^2 y^2$$

so the function $x \longmapsto x^2$ $(x \in R)$ and the binary operation of multiplication are compatible.   ■

Exercise 2

  (i) Are the function $x \longmapsto x^2$, $(x \in R)$ and the binary operation of addition on R compatible?

 (ii) Are the function

$$x \longmapsto |x| \quad (x \in R)$$

and the binary operation of (a) addition, (b) multiplication on R compatible?

(iii) Are the function

$$x \longmapsto x_5 \text{ (the remainder when } x \text{ is divided by 5)} \quad (x \in Z)$$

and the binary operation of (a) addition, (b) multiplication on Z compatible?

(iv) What can we say about compatibility of a function with domain A and a binary operation on A, *if the function is one–one*?
(HINT: Consider the implication of the use of the word "whenever" in our definition of compatibility.)   ■

Solution 2 **Solution 2**

(i) NO: e.g. $\left.\begin{array}{l} f(2) = f(-2) \\ f(-1) = f(-1) \end{array}\right\}$ BUT $f(2 + (-1)) \neq f(-2 + (-1))$.

(ii) Compatible with multiplication only.

(iii) Compatible with addition and with multiplication.

(iv) The requirement for compatibility is always met since $f(a_1) \neq f(a_2)$ for any two distinct elements $a_1, a_2 \in A$, and $f(a_1 \circ a_3)$ has to be equal to $f(a_2 \circ a_4)$ only *whenever*

$$f(a_1) = f(a_2)$$

$$f(a_3) = f(a_4)$$

(See also the solution to Exercise 1.) ∎

We can now take the last step and show that:

> Given any function f with domain A and a compatible binary operation $\circ$, then we can define an *induced* binary operation $\square$ on $f(A)$ by
>
> $$f(a_1) \square f(a_2) = f(a_1 \circ a_2)$$

As we have seen the only thing wrong with taking Equation (1) as a definition of $\square$ is that the result of combining two elements of $f(A)$ may not be unique. This is because $f(a_1)$ may be the image of other elements of A as well; and similarly for $f(a_2)$.

Suppose

$$f(a_1) = f(a_2)$$ Equation (2)

and

$$f(a_3) = f(a_4)$$ Equation (3)

for some $a_1, a_2, a_3, a_4 \in A$; then, for uniqueness, we require

$$f(a_1) \square f(a_3) = f(a_2) \square f(a_4)$$

This implies

$$f(a_1 \circ a_3) = f(a_2 \circ a_4)$$ Equation (4)

Equations (2), (3), and (4) are just the conditions for the compatibility of f and $\circ$.

So we see that the uniqueness condition on $\square$, as defined in Equation (1), requires compatibility. Moreover, compatibility (i.e. Equations (2), (3) and (4) guarantees that $\square$, as defined in Equation (1), is a binary operation.

Now, the whole reason for wishing to define $\square$ by Equation (1) was in order that f should be a morphism from $(A, \circ)$ to $(f(A), \square)$. Thus we see that

> Compatibility of f and $\circ$ guarantees the existence of a morphism.

Example 3 **Example 3**

Set A: R^+

Binary operation $\circ$: $+$

Function f: $x \longmapsto \dfrac{1}{x}$ $(x \in A)$

This is a *one–one* function, so the compatibility requirement is automatically satisfied, and we therefore *know* that a morphism exists and that it is an *isomorphism*.

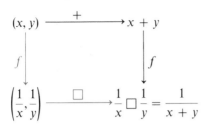

The image set in this example is the same as the domain, and so, in order to recognize □ (if we can) we need to determine $a \square b$, where a and b belong to the image set. We do this as follows:

Let

$$\frac{1}{x} = a, \qquad \frac{1}{y} = b$$

Then

$$a \square b = \frac{1}{\dfrac{1}{a} + \dfrac{1}{b}} = \frac{ab}{a + b}$$

and this gives us the rule for □.   ■

Exercise 3

Exercise 3
(5 minutes)

(i) Extend the investigation of Example 3 to obtain the rule for □ when the original binary operation ∘, is multiplication.

(ii) Investigate similarly:

Set A: R^+
Binary operation ∘: $+$
Function f: $x \longmapsto \log x \quad (x \in A)$ ■

Solution 3

(i) For multiplication, we have

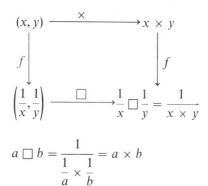

$$a \,\square\, b = \frac{1}{\dfrac{1}{a} \times \dfrac{1}{b}} = a \times b$$

i.e. the rule for $\square$ is the same as the rule for $\times$.

(ii) The log mapping is a one–one function, therefore we know that we can define $f(x) \,\square\, f(y) = f(x + y)$, i.e.

$$\log x \,\square\, \log y = \log (x + y)$$

Let

$$\log x = a$$
$$\log y = b$$

then, defined on the image set R,

$$a \,\square\, b = \log (\text{antilog } a + \text{antilog } b) \qquad\qquad \blacksquare$$

3.2.4   Units and Dimensions

The morphism idea is very important to the understanding of a unified
approach to a substantial body of mathematics. What we have developed
in this unit is only the beginning of the story. As you continue to work
through this course you will find many examples of morphisms, and we
shall also develop the concept itself further in later units. It is our experience
that the subject matter of this unit is quite difficult to grasp at first, but
as time goes by, and as it recurs again and again, you will find that the
morphism concept will be gradually assimilated.

We are concluding this unit with a brief introduction to the very important
practical topic of dimensions. We have included this topic here because
it provides us with a particularly good illustration of the morphism
concept. Because dimensions are directly related to the concept of
measurement, we begin with a short discussion of the idea of a unit of
measurement.

$$A \,\text{———————————————}\, B$$

We cannot express the length of the line AB in terms of a number alone;
for example, to say that its length is 4.5 is quite meaningless. You would
not know whether we meant 4.5 inches, 4.5 centimetres, or 4.5 times the
length of some previously given line, and even if we said "4.5 cm" (say),
this would be meaningful only if we were already agreed on what we
mean by a centimetre.

Before we can express our measurement meaningfully, then, we need to choose a *unit of length*. Our choice can be quite arbitrary, as long as it is properly defined. Two units which are in common use are the yard and the metre, and these have to be defined in terms of a *standard length*. Originally, a standard length was the distance between two parallel lines engraved on a particular bar of metal (bronze in the case of the yard, and platinum-iridium in the case of the metre). Since 1960, however, the length of the metre has been defined in terms of the wavelength of orange light emitted under specific conditions by a krypton atom of mass 86; and since 1963, the yard has been defined in terms of the standard metre. (You are not, of course, meant to memorize these details.)

Once we have our standard length, then we can repeat it along a straight line, and so obtain lengths of $2, 3, \ldots, n$ units, and we can also obtain intermediate lengths of p/q units where $p, q \in Z^+$.

We can obtain units for measuring other physical quantities in a similar manner. For example, we can define our unit of mass as the *kilogram* and our unit of time as the *second*. These two units are defined *without reference to our previously defined unit of length*, that is to say, the units of length, mass and time are all mutually *independent*.

It would be possible to choose independent units for all measurable physical quantities, but it is much more convenient, where we can do so, to choose units which are derived from the basic units of mass, length and time. For velocity, for example, we may choose as our unit the "metre-per-second", which is a unit derived from the metre as a unit of length and the second as a unit of time. By choosing our unit of velocity in this way, we ensure that an object travelling with unit velocity, travels a unit of length in a unit of time. If we now change either of the basic units, the derived unit will be changed also.

Suppose now that we have some physical quantity, ϕ (say); ϕ may be velocity, or acceleration, or force, or work, etc.* Let us suppose further that our derived unit of ϕ is to depend solely upon our assumed units of length, mass and time. (This is an assumption because, for instance, these units are inadequate for some quantities in, say, electricity.) We now define the dimensions of ϕ to be the symbols

Main Text
* *

Definition 1
* *

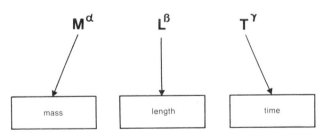

Notation 1

where α, β, γ will have numerical values which are appropriate for ϕ in a consistent set of units. (Alternatively, we can define the dimensions of ϕ to be the ordered triple (α, β, γ).)

Example 1

Example 1

Let ϕ be velocity.

Our derived unit requires that unit length is travelled in unit time, as we have already seen.

---

* The Greek letters on this page are pronounced as shown in brackets:

ϕ (phi), α (alpha), β (beta), γ (gamma).

If we increase the unit of length and keep the unit of time constant, then the new derived unit of velocity must be *increased* by the same factor. If we increase the unit of time and keep the unit of length constant, then the unit of velocity must be *decreased* by the same factor.

Our unit of ϕ is therefore in *direct ratio* to our unit of length and in *inverse ratio* to our unit of time. Hence, $\beta = 1$ and $\gamma = -1$ for ϕ, and, since mass has no influence, $\alpha = 0$. The dimensions of ϕ are thus

$$M^0 \qquad L^1 \qquad T^{-1} \qquad (\text{ or } (0, 1, -1))$$

or just LT^{-1}. ∎

Exercise 1

Exercise 1
(2 minutes)

(i) What are the dimensions of *acceleration*?
(ii) From the equation

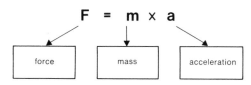

deduce the dimensions of *force*. ∎

If an equation relating various physical quantities is to be true in every system of units, then the dimensions on both sides must be the same. We can define the "multiplication" of dimensional expressions by

Main Text
* *

$$(M^\alpha L^\beta T^\gamma) \times (M^{\alpha_1} L^{\beta_1} T^{\gamma_1}) = M^{\alpha + \alpha_1} L^{\beta + \beta_1} T^{\gamma + \gamma_1}$$

Equation (1)

or

$$(\alpha, \beta, \gamma) \times (\alpha_1, \beta_1, \gamma_1) = (\alpha + \alpha_1, \beta + \beta_1, \gamma + \gamma_1)$$

We thus have a simple preliminary method of checking whether or not a given equation stands a chance of being correct, and also of determining the dimensions of constants of proportion which are often encountered in relations between physical quantities. This subject of dimensional analysis is a study on its own which we do not intend to discuss more than is necessary for our present purpose.

We are able to use dimensional analysis because of the *morphism* from physical quantities to their respective dimensions which preserves "multiplication".

We can represent this morphism by*

$$
\begin{array}{ccc}
(\phi, \psi) & \xrightarrow{\quad \times \quad} & \phi \times \psi \\
{\scriptstyle \dim} \downarrow & & \downarrow {\scriptstyle \dim} \\
(\dim(\phi), \dim(\psi)) & \xrightarrow{\quad \times \quad} & \dim(\phi \times \psi) = \dim(\phi) \times \dim(\psi)
\end{array}
$$

where $\phi, \psi \in P$, the set of physical quantities, and "dim" is the function which maps a given physical quantity to its dimensions.

Notation 2

Although we have $\times$ twice in this commutative diagram, neither is quite the usual $\times$ on R. The lower $\times$ is defined by Equation (1), the upper $\times$ is the combination of physical quantities such as $ma = (m \times a)$ in $F = ma$. However, we have used the symbol $\times$ rather than invent two special symbols, because there seems little likelihood of any confusion arising.

* The Greek letter ψ is pronounced "psi".

Before asking you to attempt the final exercise, we give a list of dimensions of some mechanical quantities.

P	$\dim (P)$
Quantity	*Dimensions*
Velocity	LT^{-1}
Acceleration	LT^{-2}
Force	MLT^{-2}
Work (Energy)	ML^2T^{-2}
Angle	Dimensionless
Angular Velocity	T^{-1}
Angular Acceleration	T^{-2}
Moment of Inertia	ML^2

(Here "dimensionless" means that $\dim(\text{angle}) = M^0L^0T^0$, that is the unit of angle does not depend on mass, length or time.)

Exercise 2

Exercise 2
(5 minutes)

(i) Given the equation of gravitation

$$F = G\frac{m_1 m_2}{d^2}$$

where

> F is force,
> m_1, m_2 are masses,
> d is the distance apart of the masses,
> G is a gravitational constant,

find the dimensions of G.

(ii) How should we define our unit of force so as to make G, in (i) above, identically equal to unity in all consistent systems of units?

(iii) Why is dimensional analysis alone unable to give us the numerical value of any particular constant such as G? ■

Solution 1

(i) LT^{-2} (or $(0, 1, -2)$)

(ii) MLT^{-2} (or $(1, 1, -2)$)

(Notice that, if "dim" represents the function which maps a physical quantity to its dimensions, then we have by implication used

$$\text{dim}\,(F) = \text{dim}\,(m) \times \text{dim}\,(a)$$

where $\times$ is the binary operation defined in Equation (1) on page 38.) ■

Solution 2

(i) $M^{-1}L^3T^{-2}$. Since the dimensions on both sides must be the same, we have

$$MLT^{-2} = M^\alpha L^\beta T^\gamma \frac{M^2}{L^2}$$

where the dimension of G is represented by $M^\alpha L^\beta T^\gamma$. This gives $\alpha = -1, \beta = 3, \gamma = -2$ by equating powers of M, L, T separately.

(ii) Define it as the magnitude of the forces exerted on each other by two unit masses unit distance apart.

(iii) Because the function $\text{dim}:P \longmapsto \text{dim}\,(P)$ is a homomorphism. Thus any measurement of length, e.g.

> 3 metres,
> 6 metres,
> 8 feet,
> etc.

maps simply to L, and the information contained in the numerical value is lost. ■

3.2.5 Summary

In the second part of this unit we have developed the idea of a morphism, which is defined as a function

$$f:(A, \circ) \longmapsto (f(A), \square)$$

such that $f(a_1) \square f(a_2) = f(a_1 \circ a_2)$ for *all* $a_1, a_2 \in A$.

The necessary and sufficient condition for the existence of a morphism is that f and $\circ$ should be *compatible*, i.e. whenever

$$f(a_1) = f(a_2)$$

and

$$f(a_3) = f(a_4)$$

Then

$$f(a_1 \circ a_3) = f(a_2 \circ a_4), \quad \text{where } a_1, a_2, a_3, a_4 \in A.$$

If f is a one–one function, this condition is automatically satisfied.

If f is one–one, we have an *isomorphism*.

If f is many–one and is compatible with $\circ$, we have a *homomorphism*.

Morphisms arise in many branches of mathematics and provide a unifying concept. They are also useful in permitting an alternative (and often easier) method of performing a calculation (as in the use of logarithms to simplify multiplication).

A simple, but frequently useful, example of a morphism is the "theory of dimensions", which may be used to find the "form" of a physical law when one knows the physical quantities involved.

M 100 — Mathematics

Title

Unit No. 1. Functions
2. Errors and Accuracy
3. Operations and Morphisms
4. Finite Differences
5. NO TEXT
6. Inequalities
7. Sequences and Limits (I)
8. Computing (I)
9. Integration (I)
10. NO TEXT
11. Logic (I): Boolean Algebra
12. Differentiation (I)
13. Integration (II)
14. Sequences and Limits (II)
15. Differentiation (II)
16. Probability and Statistics (I)
17. Logic (II): Proof
18. Probability and Statistics (II)
19. Relations
20. Computing (II)
21. Probability and Statistics (III)
22. Linear Algebra (I)
23. Linear Algebra (II)
24. Differential Equations (I)
25. NO TEXT
26. Linear Algebra (III)
27. Complex Numbers (I)
28. Linear Algebra (IV)
29. Complex Numbers (II)
30. Groups (I)
31. Differential Equations (II)
32. NO TEXT
33. Groups (II)
34. Number Systems
35. Topology
36. Mathematical Structures